BETTY JO'S FAMOUS COWBOY COOKIN'

Betty Jo & Booger Brown

Special thanks to my son, Gary
and daughter-in-law, Pam Brown.

TABLE OF CONTENTS

ranch.
recipes

"simple but
hearty"

beef stew

SERVING SIZE: 6-8 | PREP TIME: 30 MIN | COOKING TIME: 2 HOURS 30 MINUTES

INGREDIENTS

- 3 lbs. chuck roast, trimmed and cut into 2" cubes
- Salt and pepper
- ¼ cup flour
- ¼ cup vegetable oil
- 1 cup onion, chopped
- 4 cups beef stock
- 6 carrots, peeled and chopped
- 6 potatoes, peeled and quartered

PREPARATION

Season chuck roast cubes with salt and pepper and then toss in flour until lightly coated. Heat some of the oil in scalding hot cast iron pan.

Sear chuck roast cubes on all sides until brown. Do in small batches, adding more oil when necessary. Set beef aside. In the same skillet, sauté onions until translucent.

Add 1 cup of stock to deglaze and add contents of skillet, onions, and beef to a large pot. Add remaining stock, carrots, and enough water to cover. Bring to a boil. Reduce heat to medium and cook for 1 hour, stirring occasionally.

Add potatoes and cook for another 1 hour until potatoes, meat, and carrots are fork tender.

ONCE UPON A SADDLE

Back in the day, we used to butcher our own beef. It's a common thing to do around these parts, and it's one way that we'd spend time as a family. We would all load up in the Jeep, and Neal would always have Gary pick out the best, fattest heifer. One way to make good use of all that beef was to make a simple yet hearty dish like beef stew. It's a sturdy meal that could hold the boys over through their hard-working days. Even after lunch they would still have 5 or 6 hours of working to do, since cowboys work sunup to sundown, so cooking real sustaining meals is a huge part of the culinary choices we make. Beef stew, served over rice, definitely hits that mark and is one of the most common meals at roundup.

hog jowl and black-eyed peas

SERVING SIZE: 6-8 | PREP TIME: 25 MIN | COOKING TIME: 1 HOUR 30 MINUTES

INGREDIENTS

- 1 lb. black-eyed peas
- 1 lb. hog jowl (can substitute with salt pork or bacon)
- Salt and pepper to taste
- 1 onion, chopped (optional)

PREPARATION

Wash black-eyed peas and sift to remove bad peas and small stones. Drain.

Chop hog jowl into medium to large cubes and add with drained peas to a large Dutch oven or tight-lid cast iron pot.

Add water to cover and bring to a boil. Simmer for 1 hour.

Add salt and pepper to taste. Jowl will be salty so use salt sparingly.

Test peas for tenderness. Continue to add water to barely cover and simmer until tender, stirring frequently to prevent sticking. Remove from heat when peas are tender and liquid is thick.

Serve with fluffy rice.

" it's a tradition "

TASTY GOOD LUCK CHARM

This was a dish that always had to be cooked on New Year's! In this part of the country it's a tradition and a common belief that it'd bring you good luck for the coming year if you did. I'm not sure that it worked every year, but we were still always thankful for our many blessings! You can substitute salt pork or bacon for the hog jowl, but hog jowl always had a special place in our household – Neal always wanted to have it for breakfast instead of bacon or ham, or sausage like most folk. Since breakfast was his favorite meal of the day (and since his absolute favorite breakfast was hog jowl, 2 eggs over easy, and grits), you can imagine we always had it on hand. I'd highly recommend you try it first the original way!

HOW IT CAME TO BE

When Neal and I got married and started having a family, we moved to a beautiful place called Burdine Ranch. While we were there, Neal took care of the Burdine family cattle while I kept the house and raised the children. Once Gary and Joanne were old enough, I went back to working and helping out with cooking the roundups, so I had to come up with a bunch of new recipes. I came up with this recipe during our time living on that ranch. It was so tasty and always satisfying. The secret is in the pimientos and cooking with cast iron!

> " tasty and satisfying "

burdine chicken

INGREDIENTS

· 4 oz. salt pork
· 1 whole fryer chicken
· 1 ½ cups rice
· 3 cups water
· 1 can of English peas
· 1 small jar of pimientos

PREPARATION

Preheat the oven to 450°F.

In a large cast iron skillet, brown the salt pork then remove and set aside. Add chicken and brown – no need to cook all the way through.

Add rice and water to the chicken. Cover the skillet with a lid and place in the oven for 45 minutes.

Add peas, pimientos, and crumbled salt pork. Cook for an additional 15 minutes uncovered.

meat loaf

INGREDIENTS

- 8 oz. can of tomato sauce
- ¼ cup ketchup
- Salt and pepper to taste
- 1 lb. ground beef
- ¾ cup breadcrumbs (or rice*)
- 2 eggs, well beaten
- ¼ cup finely chopped onion
- ¼ cup finely chopped bell peppers

PREPARATION

Preheat the oven to 350°F.

Combine tomato sauce, ketchup, and bring to a simmer. Allow it to reduce and then remove from heat and let cool. Add salt and pepper to taste.

Mix remaining ingredients in a large bowl. Take care not to smash the breadcrumbs or overmix. Add mixture to a greased 9 × 5-inch loaf dish. Spread tomato sauce mixture over the loaf and place in oven for 1 hour until fully cooked.

Use rice instead of breadcrumbs for a fun twist.

LESSON LEARNED

Another example of how we used to use our own cattle to satisfy the hunger of the cowboys working the ranch, a great meat loaf was always welcome after a long morning of rounding up cattle (especially if the cattle were particularly difficult that day!). Getting plenty of meat is essential to the cowboy diet, so there's always a meat dish on the menu. And if there isn't, you can bet that it'll be noticed right away! Once, when cooking for the roundup, all the cowboys were gathered around the table and were digging in when, all of a sudden, Neal stopped and looked around at the table before exclaiming, "Hey! Are we going to have any meat for lunch?" I had clean forgot to put it on the table!! The men nearly fell off their seats laughing. To this day, I haven't heard the end of it!

"
essential to the
cowboy diet
"

swamp cabbage with salt pork

SERVING SIZE: 10–12 | PREP TIME: 20 MIN | COOKING TIME: 45 MIN – 1 HOUR

INGREDIENTS

· 3 swamp cabbages
· 6 oz. salt pork, diced

PREPARATION

Trim cabbage and cut into bite-sized pieces. Be careful not to use any that are too tough or bitter.

Dice salt pork into ½-inch pieces and sauté.

Place cabbage into pot, add 1 ½ inches of water. Add salt pork and cook until cabbage is tender.

" everyone loves it "

FROM THE HEART

This dish was a must at all the Brown family gatherings. Neal would go out into the woods and chop two or three swamp cabbages down and bring them home. I would cut them up and use the sweet, tender parts of the roots and the cabbage hearts. Everyone loves it (so much so that the town of LaBelle, Florida, has a Swamp Cabbage Festival every year!). This particular preparation is Christina's favorite dish. She used to go out in the woods with Neal to fetch them, and we have quite a few pictures of her up in the trees!

brown's best
baked beans

SERVING SIZE: 6-8 | PREP TIME: 15 MIN | COOKING TIME: 40 MINUTES

INGREDIENTS

· 1 onion, diced
· ¼ cup ketchup
· ¼ cup mustard
· 1 cup light brown sugar
· 3 16 oz. cans of pork and beans, undrained
· Thick-cut bacon

PREPARATION

Preheat the oven to 350°F.

Mix onion, ketchup, mustard, light brown sugar, and beans together in a casserole dish.

Layer bacon on top. Place in the oven for 30-40 minutes until bacon is crisp.

" we gotta have some beans "

A COWBOY'S MAGIC BEAN

This is an example of when the student became the teacher. My daughter-in-law, Pam, had the most delicious baked beans I'd ever tasted, so much so that she was nominated as the designated baked bean maker of the ranch roundups. Not only was it a ranch favorite, and the most often requested side, it's also a family favorite and was regularly found at home during our family BBQs. They're so good that, one time, Booger called Pam up from a BBQ he was at across the state just to ask how to cook them up because no one could make them just right! The secret is – use LIGHT brown sugar, it's the perfect flavor!

MAKES ALL THE COWBOYS GRIN

Ranch rice was a regular fixing alongside any pork dish. The flavors just blended so well. This wasn't regular rice that was served with any regular dish, this rice had a specific flavor profile that made all the cowboys grin (we even made this dish on an episode of *The Cowboy Way*). What's great is that this particular recipe can be cooked in an oven or on top of a stove. It's simple and can be thrown together with canned products that are easy to store and pack with you, so, if ever needed, we could make it on the fly in the middle of the pasture. If they had to camp out because they were too far out to drive back in time for the roundup meal, then this was something easy and delicious that could be whipped up. One of my favorite things to do was ride out into the pasture with Neal, looking at all the cattle, and getting far out into the wild on my horse. Sometimes we'd get so far that it only made sense to light a fire and have a meal right out there in the open. Ranch rice was a great and easy go-to choice to cook in a Dutch oven over a campfire!

> " easy and delicious "

ranch rice

INGREDIENTS

- 1 10.5 oz. can of onion soup
- 1 10.5 oz. can of beef broth
- 1 6 oz. can of sliced mushrooms, undrained
- 1 cup rice
- 1 stick butter, room temperature, cut into small cubes

PREPARATION

Preheat the oven to 350°F or prepare campfire.

Mix all ingredients in a small covered casserole dish and bake or hang over campfire for 1 hour until rice is tender.

chocolate
cake

INGREDIENTS

CAKE
- ½ cup butter
- 1 ½ cups sugar
- 2 eggs
- 2 oz. chocolate
- 2 cups flour
- 1 tsp. salt
- 1 tsp. baking soda
- 1 tsp. vanilla extract

ICING
- 3 oz. bitter chocolate
- ½ cup milk
- 1 cup sugar
- ⅛ tsp. salt
- ¼ cup cornstarch
- 1 tbsp. butter
- 1 ½ cups water
- 1 tsp. vanilla extract

PREPARATION

Preheat the oven to 350°F.

Whip butter, sugar, and eggs together until creamy. Dissolve 2 oz. of chocolate in ½ cup of hot water, allow to cool. Add chocolate to sugar mixture.

Sift flour, salt, and baking soda and mix with vanilla extract.

Combine both mixtures together until smooth. Pour into greased layer pans and place in the oven for 25 minutes.

Meanwhile, melt 3 oz. bitter chocolate over a double boiler (you can use a Pyrex bowl over a small pot of boiling water). Mix in ½ cup milk, 1 cup sugar, ⅛ tsp. salt, ¼ cup cornstarch, 1 tbsp. butter, and 1 ½ cups water. Remove from heat, add vanilla extract, and allow to cool, stirring occasionally.

Remove cake from oven and allow to cool. Frost with icing and serve.

SWEET THROUGH THE GENERATIONS

This is my grandmother's recipe, which has been passed down generation to generation. So good and always welcome on the table, what made this cake so special was the homemade icing. And, of course, the fact that it was always made with love. This was Gary's favorite dessert – in fact I knew if I made this cake it was a surefire way to get him to come work!

" made with love "

" a definite
favorite "

pineapple.
upside-down
cake

SERVING SIZE: 8-10 | PREP TIME: 30 MIN | COOKING TIME: 40 MINUTES

INGREDIENTS

- ½ cup butter
- 1 cup packed light brown sugar
- 1 20 oz. can of pineapple slices, undrained
- Maraschino cherries, drained and halved
- ½ cup chopped nuts
- Water
- 1 package yellow cake mix
- 3 eggs
- ⅓ cup vegetable oil

PREPARATION

Preheat the oven to 350°F.

Melt butter in 12-inch iron skillet. Remove from heat and stir in light brown sugar until it is well blended.

Drain pineapple in small colander; set aside juice. Arrange pineapple slices over sugar mixture and place half cherries in center of each pineapple slice. Sprinkle with nuts.

Combine pineapple juice with water to make 1 ⅓ cups. Combine with cake mix, eggs, and oil in a bowl. Whisk until blended and smooth.

Pour cake mixture over fruit in skillet. Place in oven and bake for 30–35 minutes. Remove from oven and allow to cool for 5 minutes.

Carefully loosen cake and invert onto a large, heat-safe plate. Best sliced and served warm.

UPSIDE DOWN IS RIGHT SIDE UP!

This is an old family recipe and cowboy roundup favorite to make, a definite favorite for dessert, and by far one of the best things to come out of a cast iron skillet! And the smell! That sweet and savory combination would attract every cowboy in sniffing distance!

peach
cobbler

SERVING SIZE: 6-8 | PREP TIME: 30 MIN | COOKING TIME: 1 HOUR

INGREDIENTS

- 4 cups of peach slices or 1 large can of peaches
- 2 cups sugar
- 1 cup flour
- 1 cup milk
- Salt
- 1 stick butter

PREPARATION

Preheat the oven to 325°F.

Place peaches in a pot and add 1 cup of sugar. Bring to a boil and reduce. Simmer until peaches are soft and sugar has caramelized.

Mix flour, 1 cup sugar, milk, and a pinch of salt together. Whisk until it is smooth.

Melt butter in baking dish and pour in the batter. Do not whisk into the butter. Pour peach mixture or canned peaches into the baking dish and place in the oven for 45-60 minutes until bubbly and delicious. Try adding apples or fruit cocktail to the peaches if desired.

A DISH FOR ALL SEASONS

This cobbler is probably one of the most common Southern desserts there is, but sometimes things are popular for a reason. We have access to peaches pretty much year-round, and the recipe is easy to reproduce. Sometimes, the simpler the recipe, the more delicious the dish is, and that's how I feel about a good ole cobbler! Once, we made a peach cobbler for a friend's birthday instead of a cake. I took it out of the oven and put a candle in it. When I turned around, the candle had completely melted because the cobbler was so hot. So don't forget to let it cool down some!

"
good ole cobbler
"

NOTHING COULD BE SWEETER

At the roundups, we would always serve sweet tea as a beverage (the cowboys were responsible for bringing their own coffee in thermoses). Now sweet tea, that's a Southern thing! The cowboys loved it after working hard all day in the hot sun, and they'd drink it by the gallon. And boy did I have to make sure that it was SWEET. I'd never hear the end of it if it wasn't!

> "southern best"

sweet tea

INGREDIENTS

· 1 family-style tea bag
· 4 cups boiling water
· 2 cups sugar
· 12 cups cold water
· Lemon

PREPARATION

Add tea bag to boiling water. Steep for at least 15 minutes.

Remove bag and pour liquid into a large pitcher containing the sugar. Stir until completely dissolved. Add cold water and allow to cool in the refrigerator.

Serve over ice with lemon.

booger's favorites

banana pudding

SERVING SIZE: 6-8 | PREP TIME: 25 MIN

INGREDIENTS

· 1 14 oz. can of condensed milk
· 1 large package of instant vanilla pudding
· 1 ½ cups cold water
· 8 oz. cream cheese
· 1 pint whipping cream
· 6 bananas, sliced and dipped in lemon juice (don't allow to sit in juice)
· ⅓ box vanilla wafers

PREPARATION

Combine condensed milk, instant pudding mix, water, cream cheese, and whipping cream into a large bowl. Beat together until smooth. Chill for at least 5 minutes. Once smooth, add bananas.

In a separate bowl, put down a layer of vanilla wafers along the outside of the bowl from top to bottom. Pour in pudding mixture.

Crumble remaining vanilla wafers on top and chill until ready to serve.

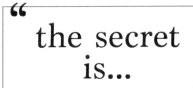

" the secret is... "

STAPLE THAT HOLDS US TOGETHER

This is a staple dessert in the Brown family, so much so that Booger requested my banana pudding be served at the rehearsal dinner for his wedding. It was always at the roundup cookouts. I can honestly say that I can't even count how many times I've made this for the boys. Gary was actually the one that perfected my recipe. It was always good, but he really made it great. The secret is in the cream cheese.

potato soup

SERVING SIZE: 6 | PREP TIME: 30 MIN | COOKING TIME: 45 MINUTES

INGREDIENTS

- 4–5 medium potatoes
- 1 stick butter
- 3 tbsp. flour
- 1 ½ cups whole milk
- Salt and pepper
- Parsley

PREPARATION

Wash and dice potatoes. Place potatoes in a pot and fill with water. Bring to a boil and cook for 30 minutes until potatoes are soft.

Melt butter in a pan and add flour. Stir well until flour is completely incorporated and cooks for at least 1 minute.

Add milk slowly while whisking. Continue until all liquid is incorporated. Add mixture to the potatoes and mix well. Bring back to a boil and then allow it to simmer for 15 minutes.

Add salt and pepper to taste and garnish with parsley when ready to serve.

MEDICINE FOR THE SOUL

This is Booger's medicine. He very much thought (and still thinks) that this soup would cure anything. One time he was dating a girl and got sick. He asked her to come over so she could learn how to cook the soup for him so he could get better! She actually showed up at our door asking for the recipe. We made some together and sent her off!

> " cure for everything "

" booger's absolute favorite "

WHO WANTS TO DATE A COWBOY?

My grandson Booger's absolute favorite meal of all time
and still his favorite to this day: classic, creamy mac
and cheese. In fact, on Booger's show, when he was still
dating, one of his dating requirements was whether or
not a girl could cook a great macaroni and cheese.

mac and cheese

INGREDIENTS

CHEESE SAUCE
- ⅓ cup powdered milk
- 1 packet gelatin
- 1 cup boiling water
- 16 oz. cheddar cheese

MAIN DISH
- 1 lb. box elbow macaroni
- Milk
- ¼ stick butter
- Salt and pepper

PREPARATION

Mix powdered milk, gelatin, and boiling water in a blender. Blend to combine. Add cheddar cheese and blend until smooth.

Grease a small loaf pan and pour cheese mixture in. Cover and chill overnight.

Boil elbow macaroni until tender. Drain but do not wash. Add a splash of milk, butter, and a splash of pasta water.

Cut cheese loaf into small cubes and add to hot pasta, stirring as you go, until fully melted. Add salt and pepper to taste and serve while hot.

pumpkin bars

INGREDIENTS

BARS
· ½ cup vegetable oil
· 1 cup sugar
· 1 cup canned pumpkin
· 2 eggs
· 1 cup self-rising flour
· 1 tsp. baking soda
· ½ tsp. salt
· 1 tsp. cinnamon

ICING
· 8 oz. cream cheese
· 1 tsp. vanilla extract
· ¾ stick butter, room temperature
· 1 tsp. cinnamon
· 1 ¾ cups powdered sugar

PREPARATION

Preheat the oven to 350°F.

Mix bar ingredients together until smooth. Pour into a greased cookie sheet or shallow cake pan and place in oven for 20–25 minutes.

While bars are baking, whisk together icing ingredients until smooth and incorporated.

Remove pan from oven and cover with an even layer of icing.

Cut into bars and serve.

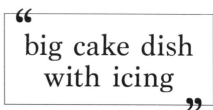

> " big cake dish
> with icing "

CAMP SNACKS TO GO!

When Booger was a little boy, he would always be going camping with his Uncle Benny (Neal's brother). Before he'd leave, he'd always stop by my house to see if I had anything he could pack and bring with them to eat. If I had any pumpkin bars, you better believe Booger would grab every last one. I used to wonder how many would actually make it to the campsite! Booger loved going camping, and he loved his Uncle Benny.

"are you hungry?"

fried
pork chops

SERVING SIZE: 1 | PREP TIME: 15 MIN | COOKING TIME: 25 MINUTES

INGREDIENTS

· 2 center cut pork
  chops
· Salt and pepper
· Self-rising flour
· Vegetable oil

PREPARATION

Salt and pepper pork chops and coat lightly in flour.

Heat oil in a cast iron skillet. Fry pork chops until golden brown on the outside and cooked through.

Optional: Set aside the pan drippings and add a couple tablespoons of flour to the skillet. Cook through then add drippings back in, scraping all the bits off the bottom of the pan. Whisk in some beef or chicken stock until smooth. Pour gravy over chops.

THE BEST FOR GUESTS

Booger would say, "This is the finest meal." And like most great things, it couldn't be simpler to make – it just requires a little practice. When he was a bachelor, this meal was the test for any woman he would date. Jaclyn, of course, made them just right! Once when Booger was young, we had company over for dinner. We all know when you have guests, you want everything to be just right, so that means having the table set with a great meal. We had fried pork chops, macaroni and cheese, and a few other of his favorites. When everyone started eating, Booger looked around at the spread and said in a loud voice, "I wish we had company every day!" It was a Brown family moment I'll never forget!

saddle-up sides

seven
layer salad

SERVING SIZE: 6-8 | PREP TIME: 15 MIN

INGREDIENTS

- ½ head lettuce, shredded
- 1 small onion, chopped
- 1 cup bell peppers, coarsely chopped
- 1 cup celery, coarsely chopped
- 1 can of peas, drained
- 1 ½ cups mayonnaise
- ½ cup parmesan cheese
- 2 tbsp. sugar
- 5 strips of bacon, cooked, drained, and crumbled

PREPARATION

Arrange half the lettuce at the bottom of a large glass bowl.

Layer onion, bell peppers, celery, peas, then remaining lettuce.

Mix mayonnaise, cheese, and sugar. Spread over the top in an even layer. Sprinkle bacon crumbles on top.

Chill in refrigerator for at least 4 hours before serving. Can be made the night before.

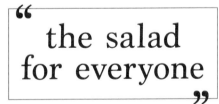

" the salad for everyone "

FRESH FARM PRODUCE

Anytime we had an occasion to have a seven-layer salad I would always have my Mama make it. It was really her specialty. I wasn't a huge salad person, but this was the one I could get the whole family to agree on. The cowboys would always appreciate the nice, crisp, cool salad to go along with their hot, hearty meals. The trick is living in a small farming town; we had access to farm-fresh produce, making every salad perfect!

pumpkin
bread

SERVING SIZE: 10–12 | PREP TIME: 25 MIN | COOKING TIME: 1 HOUR

INGREDIENTS

- ⅔ cup shortening
- 2 ¾ cups sugar
- 4 eggs
- ⅔ cup water
- 1 can of pumpkin
- 3 ½ cups flour
- 1 ½ tsp. salt
- ½ tsp. baking powder
- 2 tsp. baking soda
- 1 tsp. cinnamon
- 1 tsp. cloves
- ⅔ cup pecans
- ⅔ cup raisins

PREPARATION

Preheat the oven to 350°F.

Beat shortening and sugar until light and creamy. Mix in eggs, water, and pumpkin.

Sift together flour, salt, baking powder, baking soda, and spices. Add to pumpkin mixture and stir in nuts and raisins.

Pour batter into 2 greased loaf pans and bake for 1 hour.

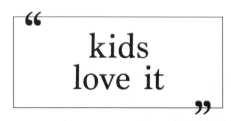

" kids love it "

LIFELONG FRIENDS

Every year, we would always load up and go out to eat on Neal's birthday. We had to go by to see Neal's old Native American friend and his family. That was the tradition. They lived on a reservation down off of Highway 41 near Copeland, Florida. When we'd visit, they would always have freshly baked pumpkin bread. That was the thing that the kids loved (and I did too). Neal's father had nicknamed his Native American friend Abraham Lincoln, and that was the name he went by! That's a true story. Neal loved to visit with Abraham Lincoln because Neal was raised with Seminoles on the reservation. He had many Seminole friends growing up, and then he moved away. Spending time with Abraham reminded him of the good old days.

"

cool, crisp, and tangy

"

A BALANCED COWBOY IS A HAPPY COWBOY

South Florida is a particularly swampy, humid place, especially during the summer. Because of the nature of ranch work, the cowboy diet is hearty and protein heavy with lots of hot dishes, meats, and potatoes. But because there were usually hot and heavy dishes served at the roundups, there always needed to be some form of cool side. Whether it was a slaw or a salad, it was always very important to balance out the meal with a cool, crisp side dish. I liked this broccoli salad recipe because it was surprisingly tangy, giving the cool side a little kick!

broccoli salad

INGREDIENTS

MAIN DISH
· 3 bunches of
  broccoli
· 1 medium red onion,
  diced
· 1 cup golden raisins
· 1 cup sharp cheddar
  cheese
· 6 slices bacon,
  cooked and
  crumbled

DRESSING
· 3 tbsp. apple cider
  vinegar
· 2-3 tbsp. sugar, to
  taste
· ¾ cup mayonnaise

PREPARATION

Mix dressing ingredients well.

Toss remaining salad ingredients together
with dressing and chill for at least an hour
before serving.

zucchini bread

INGREDIENTS

· 1 large zucchini
· 3 eggs
· 1 cup sugar
· 1 cup oil
· 1 cup brown sugar
· 2 cups flour
· 1 tsp. vanilla extract
· 1 tsp. baking power
· 1 tsp. baking soda
· 1 tsp. salt
· 3 tsp. cinnamon
· 1 cup pecans
· Raisins (optional)

PREPARATION

Preheat the oven to 350°F.

Grate zucchini with the skins. Beat eggs, sugar, and oil.

Add all ingredients together and mix well.

Split batter into two greased loaf pans and bake for 1 hour. Serve with butter.

" **delicious to munch on** "

A LOAF OF ENERGY

Sometimes I would have to go to where the cowboys were working, so I would have to cook up all the fixings for lunch, then pack and load up the buggy and travel a good 8-10 miles into the woods. Sometimes I wonder how I ever made it in one piece! When those days would happen, though, the cowboys would know if I didn't show up by noon, they'd have to come look for me. I remember one time when I got a flat and while I was waiting for the cowboys to come find me, I got hungry myself! I broke into the lunch and ate probably a whole loaf of zucchini bread. I remember thinking being stuck out here isn't so bad, as long as I have something as delicious as this to munch on!

"good to mix
things up"

gator tail

SERVING SIZE: 10 | PREP TIME: 10 MIN | COOKING TIME: 10 MINUTES

INGREDIENTS

MAIN DISH

- 1 gator tail
- 2 eggs
- 1 cup flour
- Oil

SEASONING

- 2 tsp. salt
- 1 ½ tsp. garlic salt
- 1 tsp. black pepper
- 1 tsp. onion salt
- 1 tsp. celery salt
- ½ tsp. cumin
- ¼ tsp. Creole red pepper
- ¼ tsp. garlic powder
- ¼ tsp. turmeric
- ¼ tsp. sugar

PREPARATION

Mix seasoning ingredients together well.

Pulverize gator tail with a kitchen mallet to tenderize. Cut into cubes. Sprinkle seasoning.

Whisk eggs and set in small bowl next to flour. Dip gator pieces into egg, then coat them in flour.

Heat oil in skillet and carefully fry gator pieces until golden brown and tender. Remove and allow to drain. Sprinkle a little bit of the seasoning over the fried tail and serve with your choice of dipping sauces.

GATOR REVENGE

In the town where I was raised, Everglades City, Florida, they had a festival every year that had the absolute best fried gator tail. Thousands of people would travel from all over to come and try it. Gators were a common thing on the edge of the Everglades. They weren't an everyday food for our family, but it was good to mix things up once in a while. They can be awful chewy, so a huge tip for preparing it properly is to make sure you take a small metal kitchen mallet and pulverize the meat. One year when Neal was gathering the cows, his favorite dog did not come back. When Neal went looking for her, he found a giant gator had attacked her. I don't know for sure what happened, but Neal was down at that watering hole a long time after that. He never said so, but I'm pretty sure he took care of that gator.

fried okra

INGREDIENTS

- 2 lbs. fresh-cut okra
- 1 cup buttermilk
- 1 cup plain cornmeal
- 1 cup all-purpose flour
- 1 tsp. salt
- 1 tsp. pepper
- Vegetable oil

PREPARATION

Wash okra and cut into ½-inch lengths. Discard ends. Rest okra in bowl of buttermilk.

Mix cornmeal, flour, salt, and pepper in a separate bowl and heat vegetable oil to 375 degrees in a large heavy skillet.

Dredge okra in the seasoned cornmeal and flour mixture. Fry in skillet in small batches until golden brown.

Allow okra to drain on paper towel and serve.

HARVESTING GOOD MEMORIES

Over the years, I would have friends come over, and we would go to a neighbor's garden and cut okra. I always enjoyed having my friends come over and go to the garden and work in the kitchen with me. We shared many stories and an occasional recipe, but most of all we shared laughter, which kept us all going. This Southern staple always reminds me of those times.

> " **a southern staple** "

" nothing goes to waste "

PRESERVING OUR HERITAGE

In the neighbor's garden, we always had tons of
extra okra to make pickled okra with, and all the
girls took some home. This is also my granddaughter
Christina's favorite.

okra pickled

INGREDIENTS

· Small okra pods, no longer than 3 in.
· 10-12 sterilized pint jars
· 10-12 tsp. dill seed
· 10-12 hot red peppers (optional)
· Garlic
· 2 quarts white vinegar
· 2 quarts water
· 1 cup salt

PREPARATION

Wash fresh raw okra and place vertically in sterile jars. Add 1 tsp. dill seed, 1 red pepper pod, and 1-3 cloves of garlic to each jar.

Combine vinegar, water, and salt in a pot and bring to a boil. Carefully ladle mixture into jars and seal. Allow jars to stand for several weeks before opening.

potato salad

SERVING SIZE: 6-8 | PREP TIME: 15 MIN | COOKING TIME: 25 MINUTES

INGREDIENTS

- 5 lbs. potatoes, peeled and cubed
- 8 hard-boiled eggs, chopped
- 1 red onion, sliced (optional)
- 4 stalks celery, diced
- Sweet pickles, diced
- 2 tbsp. yellow mustard
- 3 cups mayonnaise
- 1 ½ tsp. salt
- 1 ½ tsp. pepper

PREPARATION

Bring a large pot of water to a boil. Boil potatoes approximately 25 minutes until they are fork tender.

Drain and move potatoes to a large bowl and allow to cool. Add eggs, onions, celery, and sweet pickles. Mix.

Mix remaining ingredients together until smooth and fold into the bowl with potato mixture until everything is well incorporated. Cover and chill for at least 1 hour, preferably overnight, before serving.

> " **not a salad, potato salad!** "

COMMONPLACE ISN'T COMMON TASTE!

Potato salad was an easy dish to make for the cowboys. It could be made in advance and chilled. In fact, it's better if it's made early and placed in the refrigerator. It gives it the chance to really come together. Besides being a regular staple at the roundups, this was definitely a dish you would find at all the family BBQs.

cowboy casseroles

chicken enchilada
casserole

SERVING SIZE: 6—8 | PREP TIME: 25 MIN | COOKING TIME: 2 HOURS 30 MINUTES

INGREDIENTS

· 1 fryer chicken
· 1 medium onion, chopped
· 1 can of cream of chicken soup
· 1 can of cream of mushroom soup
· 1 can of chopped chiles
· Hot peppers to taste
· Corn tortillas
· 16 oz. shredded cheddar cheese

PREPARATION

Preheat the oven to 350°F.

Boil chicken in salted water until fully cooked. Allow to cool and shred chicken.

Sauté onions in butter or oil and mix in with shredded chicken, soups, chiles, and hot peppers.

Layer tortillas at the bottom of a buttered casserole dish. Add a layer of the chicken mixture and then a layer of cheese. Repeat layering until casserole dish is full.

Place in the oven and cook for 30 minutes.

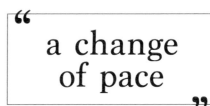

"
a change
of pace
"

PUTTING THE SOUTH IN SOUTHWEST

Every now and then we would change things up a bit and add a little variety. I can't recall exactly when I started making this dish; my best recollection is that it was from when I was younger and living in Immokalee, Florida. Somewhere along the way, I picked up this recipe and started working it in when I wanted a change of pace, and I just love it.

eggplant
casserole

SERVING SIZE: 6–8 | PREP TIME: 20 MIN | COOKING TIME: 55 MINUTES

INGREDIENTS

- 2 medium eggplants
- Salt
- 1 can of mushroom soup
- ⅓ cup milk
- 1 egg
- ½ cup onion, chopped
- 1 cup mild cheddar cheese
- 2 tbsp. butter
- ¾ cup crackers, crushed

PREPARATION

Preheat the oven to 350°F.

Boil eggplants in water until tender. Drain and mash with a potato masher. Salt to taste.

In a separate bowl, blend soup, milk, and egg. Pour mixture in with the mashed eggplant and mix well. Toss in onion and cheese to combine.

Layer mixture in a greased baking dish. Place in the oven and cook for 35–40 minutes.

Melt butter and toss with crushed crackers. Just before the dish is ready, sprinkle crackers over the casserole and continue baking until crackers are golden brown.

EGGPLANT OVERLOAD

When we lived at the Burdine Ranch, we had a neighbor who'd cultivate eggplants. He would bring over so many that I had to come up with some recipes. This is one that I came up with, and I absolutely love this dish! It's the only way I could get my grandson Booger to eat eggplant. Crumbling crackers over top of it is what gives this the soft crunch it needs.

" best way to eat eggplant "

" a special event classic "

FALL-ING FOR A SWEET CLASSIC

This is a dish we'd always prepare for special occasions.
It's got a particularly fall-style flavor and color, but
also, it's a great alternative to having regular potatoes.
You can never get enough carbs in these cowboys! It's
always served on Thanksgiving and Christmas but also
any other special event. The ooey-gooey marshmallow
topper really sells this one. In fact, the dish leans more
sweet than savory, and sometimes people will save it
for dessert.

sweet potato
casserole

SERVING SIZE: 6-8 | PREP TIME: 15 MIN | COOKING TIME: 1 HOUR 15 MINUTES

INGREDIENTS

MAIN DISH

· 4 cups sweet potato,
  boiled and mashed
· ⅓ cup milk
· ½ cup butter, melted
· 1 cup sugar
· 4 large eggs, beaten
· 1 tsp. vanilla extract
· Small marshmallows

TOPPING

· 1 cup brown sugar
· ½ cup pecans,
  chopped
· ¼ cup flour
· 1 ½ tbsp. butter,
  melted

PREPARATION

Preheat the oven to 350°F.

Mix sweet potato, milk, ½ cup butter, sugar, eggs, and vanilla extract together and pour into casserole dish.

Mix brown sugar, pecans, flour, and 1 ½ tbsp. butter in bowl. Toss to combine. Pour over sweet potato mixture and place in the oven for 45 minutes.

Just before removing from the oven, cover top of casserole with marshmallows and heat until marshmallows melt and brown slightly.

broccoli
casserole

SERVING SIZE: 6-8 | PREP TIME: 10 MIN | COOKING TIME: 1 HOUR 10 MINUTES

INGREDIENTS

- 3 10 oz. packages of frozen, chopped broccoli
- 1 can cream of mushroom soup
- 1 cup mayonnaise
- 1 cup sharp cheddar cheese, grated
- 2 eggs
- 1 medium onion, chopped fine
- 1 sleeve of crackers
- ¼ stick butter

PREPARATION

Preheat the oven to 350°F.

Boil broccoli until tender. Drain and give a rough chop.

Mix broccoli, soup, mayo, cheese, eggs, and onion in large bowl. Make sure everything is well mixed and covered. Pour into a greased casserole dish and place in the oven for 45 minutes.

Crush crackers and melt butter. Pour butter into crumbled crackers and toss to mix. Pour over casserole and continue to bake for an additional 15 minutes or until crust is golden brown and delicious.

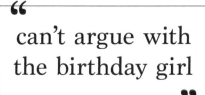

> " can't argue with the birthday girl "

HAPPY BIRTHDAY BROCCOLI!

This is my daughter-in-law Pam's favorite dish. She actually loves it so much that whenever her birthday comes around and I ask her what kind of cake she wants me to make, she just says, "How about a broccoli casserole?" How do you argue with the birthday girl? We never put any candles on it, but she loves it just the same.

dixie
desserts

"simple, quick, and delicious"

coconut cake

INGREDIENTS

YELLOW CAKE
· 1 ½ cups sugar
· ½ cup shortening
· 3 eggs
· 2 cups flour
· 3 tsp. baking powder
· 1 tsp. salt
· 1 cup buttermilk
· 1 tsp. vanilla extract

FROSTING
· 2 cups sour cream
· 2 cups sugar
· 24 oz. fresh coconut
  shavings

PREPARATION

Preheat the oven to 350°F.

Cream sugar and shortening until fluffy. Mix in eggs thoroughly. Sift flour, baking powder, and salt. Whisk dry ingredients into the egg and sugar mixture while adding buttermilk. Add vanilla extract and beat until smooth.

Pour batter into 2 greased pans. Place in the oven for 45 minutes or until cake is fully set. Remove and allow to cool. Cut each cake in half horizontally.

Mix sour cream, sugar, and coconut until fully combined. Stack the 4 cake sections and apply frosting between each layer. Completely cover the top and sides of the cake.

GOING COCO-NUTS FOR CHARITY

When I was living in South Florida, I spent a lot of my time involved in the CowBelles organization. In fact, I served as its regional president on more than one occasion. We were a group of women who cooked for the roundups, kind of like the female counterparts to the Florida Cattlemen. It was a great way to meet other ranchers and other ranchers' wives, and it allowed us to spend time getting to know each other's families. We helped each other when we could, and every year, we raised money for the organization. Each year for that fundraiser, I would make this coconut cake to be auctioned off. I used to fetch a pretty penny for this recipe; it's a real crowd pleaser. It's simple, quick, and surprisingly delicious!

cowboy cake

INGREDIENTS

MAIN DISH
· 2 cups sugar
· 2 cups flour
· 2 sticks butter
· ¼ cup cocoa
· 1 cup water
· 2 eggs
· 1 tsp. baking soda
· 1 tsp. vanilla extract
· ½ cup buttermilk

ICING
· 1 stick butter
· ¼ cup cocoa
· 6 tbsp. milk
· 1 lb. powdered sugar
· 1 cup pecans
· 1 tsp. vanilla extract

PREPARATION

Preheat the oven to 400°F.

Sift sugar and flour into a bowl. Combine 2 sticks butter, ¼ cup cocoa, and water in a saucepan and bring to a boil. Pour over sugar and flour, mix well.

Beat eggs and add to mixture along with baking soda, vanilla, and buttermilk. Pour into a greased pan and bake in the oven for 20 minutes.

Mix 1 stick butter, ¼ cup cocoa, and milk in a small pot and bring to a boil. Remove from heat and then mix in the powdered sugar, nuts, and vanilla thoroughly.

Remove cake from oven and spread icing while cake is still warm.

A CAKE FIT FOR A COWBOY

I've heard this called a Mississippi mud cake, but I call it the Cowboy Cake. This is definitely my son Gary's favorite and any chocolate lover's delight! The pecans used in this cake are a nice surprise and set it off. Doesn't everyone love chocolate and pecans?!

> " any chocolate lover's delight "

" fall, crisp smell "

AS AMERICAN AS APPLE CAKE

Something about this cake is just heavenly to the nose.
The fresh apples and the cinnamon would just fill
the house with this divine aroma. Even though South
Florida and Alabama are not known for their apples,
every once in a while, I'd just get an overwhelming
desire to make the house smell like fall. It honestly
might be the main reason I loved to make this recipe.
Well, that and the taste!

fresh
apple cake

INGREDIENTS

- 2 cups sugar
- 3 eggs
- 1 ½ cups oil
- 2 cups flour
- 1 tsp. cinnamon
- ½ tsp. salt
- 1 tsp. baking soda
- 3 cups apples, diced
- 1 cup pecans, chopped
- ¾ cup candied cherries
- 1 cup coconut
- 2 tsp. vanilla

PREPARATION

Preheat the oven to 325°F.

Cream sugar and eggs. Add oil slowly and beat well.

Sift flour, cinnamon, salt, and baking soda. Stir into egg mixture.

In a separate bowl combine apples, pecans, cherries, coconut, and vanilla extract. Mix with batter and pour into a greased and floured Bundt pan.

Bake in the oven for 1 hour 15 minutes. Remove and rest.

sour
orange pie

INGREDIENTS

- 4 eggs
- ½ cup sugar
- 1 cup sour orange juice
- 1 uncooked pie shell

PREPARATION

Preheat the oven to 325°F.

Separate egg whites and yolks. Beat egg whites until stiff and add sugar. Fold in beaten egg yolks and mix in juice.

Pour mixture into pie shell and bake until firmly set.

> ## a pretty sweet tang

A FACE-PUCKERING PIE

Sour oranges are common to South Florida swamps, and boy are they sour! This isn't the most well-known or popular dessert. Sour oranges are a bit of an acquired taste, but the cowboy way is to live off the land, and we had plenty of sour oranges to work with. Neal actually liked them in a lemonade-style beverage that the locals actually called "panther pee" because of how sour it was. Most people find it hard to drink but he loved it.

"one salty
pie..."

key lime pie

INGREDIENTS

CRUST
- ½ box of graham crackers
- ⅓ cup butter, melted
- ⅓ cup sugar

FILLING
- 3 eggs, separated into whites and yolks
- 14 oz. sweetened condensed milk
- ½ cup key lime juice
- 1 pinch cream of tartar
- ⅓ cup sugar

PREPARATION

Preheat the oven to 350°F.

Crush graham crackers into fine crumbs. Mix in melted butter and sugar. Press into pie pan and bake in the oven for 8-10 minutes. Set crust aside to cool.

Whisk egg yolks until fluffy. Add condensed milk slowly while continually whisking until thick. Add lime juice and mix lightly until combined. Pour mixture into crust and bake for 10-15 minutes or until filling sets.

While pie is baking, beat egg whites until foamy. Add cream of tartar and sugar. Beat until you have stiff peaks.

Remove pie from oven. Spread egg white mixture over pie and chill until ready to serve.

THE SALTY MISTAKE

One summer I was cooking for the cowboy roundup and I had decided to make a special key lime pie instead of the typical fruit cobbler. I remember that pie came out extra beautiful. It looked so good when I put it down on the table! All the cowboys remarked on how pretty it was and how they couldn't wait to try it. After I left to go back to work, I realized I had used salt instead of sugar. The boys talked about that salty pie for years. In fact, some people still like to tease me about that pie! As long as you don't switch up the salt and sugar, it'll taste as good as it looks.

pecan pie

SERVING SIZE: 6 | PREP TIME: 10 MIN | COOKING TIME: 1 HOUR

INGREDIENTS

- 3 eggs
- 1 cup light brown sugar
- 1 cup light corn syrup
- 3 tbsp. melted butter
- 1 tsp. vanilla extract
- 1 cup pecans
- 3 tbsp. flour
- 1 unbaked pie crust

PREPARATION

Preheat the oven to 350°F.

Mix all ingredients together well. Pour into pie crust and bake in the oven for 1 hour. Remove and allow to cool fully before slicing.

" always a crowd pleaser "

PECANS APLENTY

Growing up in Florida, one of the ingredients that was hard to get a hold of was pecans. When I finally moved to Alabama, all of that changed for me. Alabama is known for pecans! They're so plentiful here, it opened up a whole new world of pecan recipes for me. This is one of my favorite things to make, very simple, easy, and always a crowd pleaser. Even though it was simple to make, it still took a lot of work, because I would pick my own pecans, take them to get them cracked, and then clean them. All that work before I even turned on the oven!

STRAWBERRIES GALORE

We used to go to the strawberry festival every year, and we'd come home with flats and flats of fresh, juicy strawberries. Neal's brother Percy also grew them, so there was never a shortage in the house. And who doesn't like a fresh strawberry pie?

" fresh, juicy
strawberries "

strawberry pie

INGREDIENTS

- 2 quarts fresh strawberries
- 3 cups sugar
- 3 cups water
- 9 tbsp. cornstarch
- 6 tbsp. corn syrup
- 1 ½ packs of strawberry Jell-O
- 1 deep-dish pie crust, baked

PREPARATION

Mash ½ of the strawberries in a pot with the sugar. Add ½ of the water and bring to a boil. Mix remaining water, cornstarch, corn syrup, and strawberry Jell-O. Add to strawberry and sugar mixture and reduce heat to a simmer. Cook for 10 minutes until properly thickened.

Place remaining strawberries in pie crust. Pour strawberry sugar mixture over fresh strawberries and place pie in refrigerator to cool and set overnight.

buttermilk pie

INGREDIENTS

- 3 eggs
- 1 ½ cups sugar
- ¼ cup butter, melted
- 1 cup buttermilk
- 3 tbsp. flour, heaping
- 1 tsp. vanilla extract
- 1 9" deep-dish pie shell

PREPARATION

Preheat the oven to 350°F.

Blend all ingredients together until smooth. Pour mixture into the pie shell and bake for 50–60 minutes until pie is golden brown and the center is firm.

> " a simple family recipe "

LIVING OFF THE LAND

This is a classic ranch-style dessert. It's also called the "poor man's pie." In the old days, and on the ranch, you really did live off the land, and you made things with what you had. And as farmers, ranchers, and cattlemen, you had buttermilk. So, somebody figured out how to make it into something sweet to eat. This was Neal's dad's favorite pie. It's an old, nice, and simple family recipe.

guava jelly

SERVING SIZE: 6 1/2 PINTS | PREP TIME: 5 MIN | COOKING TIME: 30 MINUTES

INGREDIENTS

- 5 cups guava juice
- ¼ cup lime juice
- 7 cups sugar
- 1 ¾ oz. fruit pectin
- Mason jars with lids

PREPARATION

Mix fresh guava juice, lime juice, and sugar in a saucepot and bring to a boil. Reduce and allow to simmer for 10-12 minutes or until the mixture is thick and drops from a spoon in a jelly texture.

Add fruit pectin and bring to a boil. Simmer for an additional 10-15 minutes.

Add mixture to jars and seal. Allow to cool and set before using.

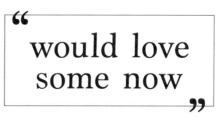

> **" would love some now "**

WHATEVER'S IN SEASON

This jelly was one thing that was easy to fix, and all the cowboys loved it. I could go out in the pastures and find a guava tree and pick the ripe ones to use for the jelly that day. When you live so far from a store, you learn to live off the land. Whatever was in season, that's what we were making. You can do this with pretty much any fruit you can get your hands on, but trust me, try some guava jelly and butter on a hot biscuit. It doesn't get any better than that!

banana
split pie

SERVING SIZE: 6 | PREP TIME: 20 MIN | COOKING TIME: 20 MINUTES

INGREDIENTS

CRUST
· 1 stick butter
· 1 ½ cups flour
· 1 cup pecans, finely chopped

FILLING
· 16 oz. cream cheese
· ½ lb. butter
· 1 lb. confectioners' sugar

TOPPING
· 6–8 bananas
· 1 can of crushed pineapple, drained
· 1 cup whipped topping
· Chocolate syrup
· Maraschino cherries

PREPARATION

Preheat the oven to 350°F.

Melt 1 stick of butter and mix with flour and pecans. Press into the bottom of a deep-dish pie pan. Bake in the oven for 20 minutes and allow to cool fully.

Beat cream cheese, ½ lb. butter, and confectioners' sugar into a smooth mixture and pour into the crust. Chill pie to allow filling to set.

Slice bananas and add them to the top of the pie. Then top with pineapple. Add whipped topping and drizzle with chocolate syrup. Add cherries, slice, and serve.

THE GRANDMA SPECIAL

This is the dessert that I'm most well known for, by far. It's a fun confection to make, and if I get invited to a party, this is most likely what I'll bring, since everyone loves it. It's different from most pies and is very rich, so even the hardiest cowboy only needs a small slice.

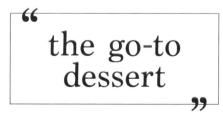

" the go-to dessert "

66

never enough chocolate

99

CAN'T HAVE TOO MUCH OF A GOOD THING

Well, here we are again with chocolate! If you're like us, you know that chocolate is always going to be a favorite dessert, regardless of how it's made. This is especially true for the Browns! You don't need fancy techniques and a million ingredients to make something great. A proper chocolate pie will always bring a family together and bringing together family is one of the best things that food can do!

chocolate pie

INGREDIENTS

· 4 cups milk
· 1 ½ cups sugar
· 2 sticks butter
· 2 tsp. salt
· ⅔ cup cornstarch
· 2 tbsp. unsweetened
  cocoa powder
· 1 tsp. vanilla extract
· 6 eggs, separated
· Pie shell

PREPARATION

Preheat the oven to 350°F.

Bring milk to 180°F. Stir constantly and do not allow to reach a full boil. Remove from heat and allow to cool.

Combine sugar, butter, salt, cornstarch, cocoa, vanilla extract, and well-beaten egg yolks. Add milk slowly, stirring constantly. Heat mixture and stir until thick and smooth.

Pour mixture into pie shell and place in the oven for 20 minutes. Remove and allow to cool and set.

bread
pudding

INGREDIENTS

· 3 cups milk
· 8 slices of bread, torn by hand into approx. 1–2 inch pieces
· ¾ cup sugar
· 3 eggs
· ½ tsp. salt
· ½ cup raisins
· 1 tsp. vanilla extract

PREPARATION

Preheat the oven to 350°F.

Bring milk to 180 degrees. Stir constantly and do not allow to reach a full boil. Remove from heat and allow to cool.

Fit bread into buttered 6 × 12-inch baking pan. Blend milk, sugar, eggs, salt, raisins, and vanilla until smooth.

Place in the oven for 45 minutes. Serve warm or at room temperature.

> " neal's absolute favorite "

THE WAY TO A HARDY MAN'S HEART

Once, Neal and I were putting mineral out for the cows when our buggy broke down six miles from home. Gary was a child at that time, and one of us had to get down to the school bus stop, an additional five miles away, to pick him up. There was a lot of work to do that day, but I had to leave Neal to finish up by himself so I could walk back to the house and grab a truck to drive to the bus stop. I made it just in time! When we got home, I decided to make Neal some bread pudding, his absolute favorite, since he had to do all the work himself that day. When he tucked into his plate you could tell he forgot all about his hard day. They say the way to a man's heart is through his stomach, and that's especially true for the Brown family!

Made in the USA
Columbia, SC
07 November 2024

45593866R00058